Thank you for helping us
Shape our common future

Steve Gundy

Tony Bancluu

Royal Roads

A Celebration

THE CASTLE, WINTER

ROYAL ROADS

A Celebration

MAURICE ROBINSON · BEVERLEY HALL · PAUL PRICE

NATURAL LIGHT PRODUCTIONS
VICTORIA, BRITISH COLUMBIA, CANADA
1995

FIFTIETH ANNIVERSARY PARADE PRACTICE, 1990

ROYAL ROADS
A Celebration

MAURICE ROBINSON · BEVERLEY HALL · PAUL PRICE

NATURAL LIGHT PRODUCTIONS
VICTORIA, BRITISH COLUMBIA, CANADA
1995

Natural Light Productions
5135 Sandgate Road
Victoria, B.C. Canada v9b 5t7

CANADIAN CATALOGUING IN PUBLICATION DATA

Robinson, Maurice
    Royal Roads: A Celebration

    ISBN 0-9699430-0-8

    1. Royal Roads Military College – Pictorial works   2. Royal Roads
Military College – History   3. Hatley Park (Victoria, B.C.) – Pictorial
works   4. Victoria (B.C.) – Buildings, structures, etc. – History
I. Hall, Bev.   II. Price, Paul E.   III. Title
U444.V6L1 1995   355'.0071171   C95-910342-2

Published with assistance from the national and local bodies of
the Ex-Cadet Club of Canada.

Bev Hall photos © Beverley D. Hall
Maurice Robinson photos © Natural Light Productions
Paul Price photos © Cromwell-Price Publishing
RRMC Archives photos, with permission of photographer Darren Oxner

Edited by Camilla Turner
Design and typesetting by Arifin A. Graham, Alaris Design
Map by Rob Struthers
Colour separations, printing and binding by Hemlock Printers Ltd.

Printed and bound in Canada

Contents

FIFTIFTH ANNIVERSARY PARADE PRACTICE, 1990

Foreword

THIS BOOK REPRESENTS a labour of love, reflected generously in inspiring photographs expressing the very essence of Royal Roads Military College over the past fifty-five years.

Dr. Maurice Robinson has masterfully assembled a wonderful collection of distinctive photographs of College life and, more importantly, of those special moments that too few cadets, staff and visitors have ever had enough time to enjoy.

I would ask that you take that precious time now, while you examine each image and turn each page. Try to imagine the moment as it has been captured here by the lens, and reflect on what it signifies and how it contributes to this story.

The quotes chosen to assist you in this journey of reflection on the ambience of Royal Roads have been carefully selected to help you better appreciate the wonder of this site and the special qualities of those who have been privileged to serve here.

The closing of Royal Roads Military College is indeed the end of an era, one based on excellent academic instruction and professional military training. The importance of this College to Canada will live on through the memories of its faculty, staff and cadets.

As we cross the threshold to a new future for Royal Roads, we all hope that this natural historic treasure will never be lost. I believe this book will not only help each of us remember what the charm and character of Royal Roads was really like, but that it will also give us a perspective to ensure that its beauty will not be significantly changed.

Thanks to the three photographers and all those who worked with them in creating this truly magnificent photographic celebration of Royal Roads.

D. B. BINDERNAGEL
CAPTAIN(N)
COMMANDANT
MAY 1995

Introduction

THE FEBRUARY 1994 ANNOUNCEMENT that the federal government would close Royal Roads Military College in June 1995 marked the end of an era.

For almost fifty-five years behind its iron-clad grey stone wall and guarded entrance, Royal Roads has trained and educated young men and, since 1984, young women, for service as officers in the Canadian Armed Forces. Though the gardens are open year-round, the hundreds of acres of ponds, pasture and woodlands of Hatley Park estate, which encompasses the military college, have all these years continued as one of Canada's best-kept secrets.

The visitor who has the temerity to leave the busy highway and venture through the gate meets an unparalleled vista. On a clear morning, a castellated tower appears through the trees against a backdrop of the Juan de Fuca Strait and the snow-capped peaks of the Olympic Mountains to the south. For those of us who have had the privilege of being associated with Royal Roads, this astonishing beauty as we hurry to work in the morning has often caught us by surprise. Sunrise and storm fronts cast their spell on the sea and mountains in an ever-changing play of light, and one can't help but reflect on how fortunate we have been to have had the opportunity of simply being here in all seasons and all weathers.

At first, it seems ironic that military practice should be exercised in such a peaceful environment. "I can look out of my window," said Officer Cadet Nasmith recently, "and see ships on the ocean, mountains across the border, a castle and gardens, a forest, deer and peacocks. Where else would I want to go to school?" Where else indeed? In the long run, however, training for a military career in such an idyllic setting may ultimately provide a subtle but important balance in the lives of many Canadian officers, who are increasingly likely to be involved in the difficult art of peacekeeping in the most heart-breaking and frustrating trouble spots on earth.

This photographic essay is a contemporary celebration of some of the finest aspects of Royal Roads, Hatley Castle, the gardens and old-growth forest through the seasons. It is drawn from the work of three photographers. Beverley Hall has been involved as a research assistant at Royal Roads for the past twelve years. Photography is one of her passions, and she has won local, national and international recognition for her work. Paul Price is a partner in Cromwell Price Publishing and has spent many hours taking pictures of the castle and gardens. His love of the estate initiated the production of this book. My own photographic accomplishments are modest, but I believe that Royal Roads is a very special place and hope that my images convey that feeling.

Readers interested in an historical overview of the military college itself are directed to the excellent text by Dr. Peter J. S. Dunnett, a professor and Dean at RRMC, *Royal Roads Military College 1940-1990: A Pictorial Retrospect*, published in 1990 by RRMC. An illustrated anthology pertaining to Hatley Park and the Dunsmuirs, covering the period before 1940, is being prepared by the Friends of Hatley Park Society.

This collection could have been expanded in a number of directions. A section on the current staff and faculty, which more properly forms part of the yearbook, has not been included here, and the contemporary cadets serve to represent those who have graduated before them.

Over the years, the faculty and staff who have played significant roles in the education and training of the cadets have also been inexorably drawn into the extended family of Royal Roads.

OFFICER CADETS ON PARADE

As a result, sentiments and memories they have recounted recently echo a familiar ring. They are perhaps best summed up by the words of a former Director of Cadets, LCol(Ret'd) Dennis McCarthy: "The atmosphere or ambience remains something that I felt and responded to as a cadet and as a staff member – something that was generally not expressed in words but was apparent in the positive if not cheerful spirit or attitude of those who studied and worked there, at all levels. It simply made one feel good to be part of it. Even in more recent years, despite the uncertainties, this perception – which is more of a sensation or experience – has prevailed." As we work here, we glance at what is around us, appreciate it momentarily and return to our schedules and preoccupations. It sustains us. The ambience is best described as the spirit of Royal Roads, and it is that which we hope will be evident in the images we present here.

We begin with a salute to the cadets, who are, as BGen V. M. Caines has said, "the embodiment of the very best of Canadian youth." Having come to Royal Roads from all sectors of society and all parts of Canada, they have worked and trained hard. They have overcome many hardships, working individually and as members of a team. During their tenure, they live by Nelson's dictum, which is etched above the entrance of Grant Block, the academic building: "Duty is the great business of a sea officer; all other considerations must give way to it however painful it is."

The cadets' boundless energy and enthusiasm on the playing fields or parade square – and sometimes even in the classroom – have always been a pleasure to observe; their appearance and public presence is not only a credit to them but a tribute to their officers and professors. When the cadets march off the parade square for the last time upon graduation, the College motto – "Truth, Duty, Valour" – shines from every face. The bonds they have formed will certainly last a lifetime, as will the vigorous training of body and mind: *Mens sana in corpore sano*. The spirit of Royal Roads has already pervaded their lives and will live on in them, whether they pursue a military career or become leaders in other fields of endeavour.

JAPANESE GARDEN IN AUTUMN

As a national heritage site, Hatley Castle itself deserves much more of an in-depth treatment than we can present here. Designed by Samuel Maclure to suggest a 15th-century castle, the palatial home is magnificent. Names of the goddesses of the seasons are inscribed in several of the rich stained glass windows that were created in England. Two grand staircases lead from the Great Hall to a minstrels' gallery above. Ivory, mother-of-pearl and ebony inlays decorate mahogany, slashed fir and cedar panelling in the main rooms. Maclure's love of fine woods shows again in doors of dark oak and hallways panelled in golden oak.

In spite of working at the College, I was amazed at the artistry of the windows, tiles, sculptured stonework, grates, doorplates and other detailing we found while preparing this book. Craftsmanship I had taken for granted for twenty-two years jumped out in startling clarity through the camera lens. Future visitors will find much to discover, and we hope this book will entice them to begin that particularly satisfying process.

The Italian, Japanese and rose gardens are much more familiar to the general public than the rest of Hatley Park estate, particularly to those who are horticultural enthusiasts. Created largely between 1908 and 1916 for the pleasure of the Dunsmuirs, the gardens are a collection of exotic and native plants, shrubs and trees. The well-tended grounds have matured during the intervening decades, and they contribute richly to Victoria's reputation as the City of Gardens.

Thirty or more labourers worked on the original estate, but in recent years, only a handful of committed gardeners have tended and nurtured the legacy of aching backs and prescient design. The Italian Garden, which has been modified over the years, has recently been restored to its former state. An immense old wisteria and intertwining clematis trail over the central loggia. Four statues representing the seasons stand amid clusters of fragrant flowers or under occasional caps of snow. Designed and planted by a landscape architect and gardener from Japan, the Japanese Garden's colours and forms emerge, peak and recede through the cycles of the year. Small streams and sinuous footpaths lead the visitor past stone lanterns and a waterwheel toward quiet arbors. Strategically placed benches and alcoves invite a pause for reflection, and many a student has found peaceful respite here from the pressures of rigorous routine.

By contrast, many parts of the densely forested grounds have remained largely undisturbed, mysterious even to cadets and faculty who have been at the College for years. This may change in time because the forest has in recent years been made much more accessible by a documented system of walking trails. In shady places on the cool forest floor, mosses and a dense carpet of needles muffle hikers' footsteps; fungi grow in the leaf litter and on decaying deadfall. Wildflowers grow in abundance in their seasons on sunlit rocky outcrops and in the more open spaces. Moss-covered limbs of western maple glow emerald green in morning light, and hollow trunks are home to pileated woodpeckers and horned owls. Even though the forest was selectively logged by the Dunsmuirs to provide fuel for the castle, greenhouse and conservatory, it still harbours cedar, fir and hemlock of great stature. They remain as testimony to the careful logging practices of earlier times.

GREAT BLUE HERON

On the northern boundary, Colwood Creek emerges from under the highway and pours over a waterfall during spring flood in its rush to Esquimalt Lagoon and the sea. Waterfowl nest in the alder groves and skunk cabbage lining the water's edge or in the bullrushes bordering the estuary. A great blue heron, disturbed from its midday repast in a quiet backwater, rises like a spectre – *grark, graark, graaark* – and seeks sanctuary in the canopy above. Cutthroat trout in autumn stream-pools linger undisturbed, and ethereal ice sculptures around the waterfall during a hard winter frost emerge and melt unwatched.

The 650 acres comprising the whole of this property represent an incredibly rich and diverse ecosystem which, for the moment, continues to flourish in the middle of a growing urban and suburban community. We must surely nurture and preserve this ecosystem for future generations; it is intact and cannot be created again. The secrets we are sharing with you in these pages are yours to discover for yourself. Tread softly when you wander through, and be at peace. You will feel, as so many of us have, the spirit of Royal Roads.

DR. MAURICE G. ROBINSON
PROFESSOR, DEPARTMENT OF CHEMISTRY
ROYAL ROADS MILITARY COLLEGE
MAY 1995

The College

IF SOMEONE HAD TOLD ME FOUR YEARS AGO THAT I WOULD BE EXPECTED TO RUN A
FORCED MARCH, JUMP OFF A CLIFF, SPEND COUNTLESS HOURS PRACTISING PRECISION
DRILL, WRITE EIGHT EXAMS IN A ROW, ORGANIZE A FORMAL BALL AND ENDURE A
YEAR MARCHING TO THE BATHROOM, I LIKELY WOULD NEVER HAVE COME TO ROADS.
OF COURSE, THEY PROBABLY WOULD HAVE FORGOTTEN TO MENTION I WOULD
MAKE SOME OF THE BEST FRIENDS I'VE EVER HAD AND THAT, WITH THEM,
ALMOST ANYTHING IS TOLERABLE.

19464 Officer Cadet Danielle Rose
1991-95

INTRAMURAL FLAG FOOTBALL

INTRAMURAL TUG-OF-WAR

SIGN IN GYMNASIUM

The rugby field is where some of my most heartfelt memories lie. It was a place where the real meaning of team spirit and character were developed. In rain, snow or sunshine, the cadets often battled against teams with far more raw talent, but not with more heart or determination.

DR. G. MAURICE LANCASTER
PROFESSOR AND DEAN OF SCIENCE, 1960-95

RUGBY

RUGBY

NELSON'S DICTUM

NEPTUNE STEPS AND GRANT BLOCK

CORONEL MEMORIAL LIBRARY

CHEMISTRY AND COMPUTER CLASSES

Horrors! The entire class was sitting at attention. No one had prepared me for this and the sobering thought passed through my mind that, unless I found the magic word, they would stay like that forever. Fortunately, with what I thought was remarkable initiative, a cadet roared, "At ease!" The class began, and I continued for the next twenty-eight years relying on cadet initiative.

DR. M. RON BARR
PROFESSOR OF CHEMISTRY, 1967-95

OCEANOGRAPHY FIELD TRIP,
GULF ISLANDS

PHYSICS LABORATORY

MILLWARD WING, NIXON BLOCK

OFFICER CADETS, DINING HALL

QUARTERDECK SET FOR CHRISTMAS LUNCHEON

EXAMINATIONS, GYMNASIUM

COLLEGE SAILBOATS, ESQUIMALT LAGOON

EVENING RITUAL: LOWERING THE FLAG AT SUNSET

Royal Roads has awakened in me a sense of purpose, of direction. It has taught me that success is achievable only through dedication and perseverance.

20981 OFFICER CADET JASON A. TOTH
1993-95

GRANT BLOCK, MAIN ENTRANCE

STAINED GLASS, THE QUARTERDECK

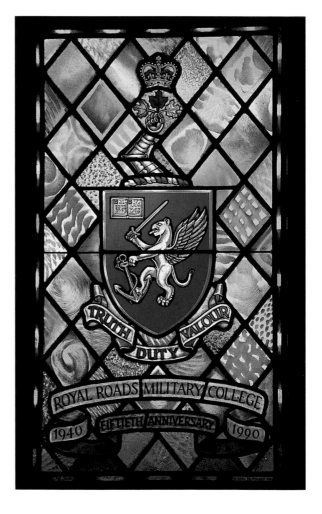

STAINED GLASS, CHAPEL, GRANT BLOCK

Above, right and previous page: NAVY DAY PARADE

I've had the chance to fly over the college in a Tudor jet, in CF-18 fighters and now, four hundred kilometres up, in the space shuttle. I had heard that perspective changes after graduation but, as a recruit there, I only dreamed it would take me so high.

MAJ CHRIS HADFIELD, ASTRONAUT
13738 OFFICER CADET, RRMC 1978-80

FREEDOM OF THE CITY OF VICTORIA PARADE

SUNSET PRACTICE AND OLYMPIC MOUNTAINS

CROQUET PLAYER AND OBSERVERS, GRADUATION WEEK

CONVOCATION

SUNSET CEREMONY: EN ROUTE TO PARADE SQUARE

SUNSET CEREMONY: EN ROUTE TO PARADE SQUARE

PARADE SQUARE, SUNSET CEREMONY

The life, heart and soul of Royal Roads Military College came from the people: healthy cadets, full of enthusiasm and vigorous spirits, and the dedicated staff, with undiminished loyalty and imaginative versatility.

DR. PETER SMART
PROFESSOR OF MATHEMATICS, 1967-89

Above: OFFICER CADET AT SUNSET CERMONY; *next page:* GUN CREW, SUNSET CEREMONY

SUNSET CEREMONY

BAND AT GRADUATION PARADE

GRADUATION: ACADEMIC PROCESSION

GRADUATION PARADE, REVIEWING THE GRADUATES

GRADUATES SALUTING GUEST OF HONOUR

GRADUATES LEAVING PARADE SQUARE

CONGRATULATIONS!

Like those warriors of an earlier time, all this that was Royal Roads
passes away, but its spirit in a grand cause lives on in what it has
given to those who build tomorrow's traditions. In after-years,
one of those chance encounters – "You may not remember me, sir,
but..." – will summon pride in what we all achieved together.

MAJ(RET'D) G. W. STEPHEN BRODSKY
SPECIAL LECTURER IN ENGLISH, 1973-76

TEA ON THE CASTLE LAWNS AFTER GRADUATION

Next page: THE CASTLE IN MORNING MIST

The Castle

THE SANDSTONE WAS BROUGHT FROM NEIGHBOURING VALDEZ AND SATURNA ISLANDS,

WHILE THE ANDESITE CAME FROM HADDINGTON ISLAND. INSIDE THE HOUSE,

ROSEWOODS, TEAK AND OAK WERE USED TO CREATE AN ATMOSPHERE OF LUXURY

AND SUMPTUOUSNESS. THE SOLID OAK DOORS, THE LARGE SANDSTONE FIREPLACE, THE

AUSTRALIAN MAHOGANY IN THE DOWNSTAIRS PORTION, THE OAK PANELLING, THE

IMPORTED STAINED GLASS WINDOWS AND PEWTER FITTINGS, THE HUGE CHANDELIERS

AND THE ENCLOSED CIRCULAR STAIRCASE RARELY FAIL TO IMPRESS VISITORS.

Dr. Peter J. S. Dunnett

PROFESSOR OF ECONOMICS AND DEAN OF ARTS, 1974-95

IN ROYAL ROADS MILITARY COLLEGE 1940-1990: A PICTORIAL RETROSPECT

Clockwise from upper left: FOUNTAIN AND ORNAMENTAL POND; THE CASTLE; WATER LILY
Next page: VIEW OF THE CASTLE FROM LOWER LAWNS

It might have been our home.

THE QUEEN MOTHER

As conveyed to Midshipman Peers in 1947 aboard *HMS Vanguard*, in transit from Britain to South Africa. Capt(RCN) R. C. K. Peers later became Commandant of Royal Roads (1970-76). The King and Queen had made a clandestine visit to Hatley Castle in 1939. The British government apparently considered it to be a suitable refuge for the Royal Family during World War II.

AUTUMN

WINTER

CASTLE AND NEPTUNE STEPS, SUMMER AND WINTER

PEACOCK AND NEPTUNE STEPS

STATUETTE, THE NEPTUNE STEPS

THE NEPTUNE FOUNTAIN

NEPTUNE STEPS, SPRING: LIONS AND STATUETTE

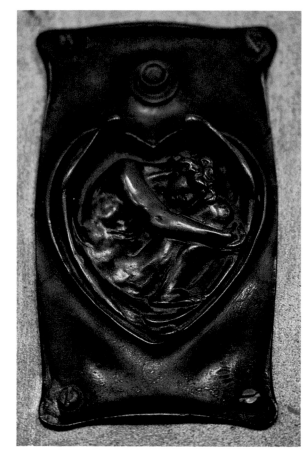

Left and right: DETAIL OF STONEWORK, CASTLE ENTRANCE; *middle:* THE DOORBELL

In the first decades of the 20th century, it was the centre of Victoria social life with grand balls, parties and dinners. The most famous guest was probably His Royal Highness the Prince of Wales, grandson of Queen Victoria, but all the Governors-General of the day were entertained at the Castle.

DR. PETER J. S. DUNNETT
PROFESSOR OF ECONOMICS
AND DEAN OF ARTS, 1974-95
IN *ROYAL ROADS MILITARY COLLEGE
1940 1990: A PICTORIAL RETROSPECT*

THE GREAT HALL

WINDOWS, THE GREAT HALL

Clockwise from upper left: CEILING, GREAT HALL;
BANNISTERS AND DOORWAY, GREAT HALL;
GREAT HALL AND FIREPLACE; THE ANTE-ROOM

FLAGS OF THE THREE SERVICES, GREAT HALL

STAINED GLASS, SENIOR STAFF MESS

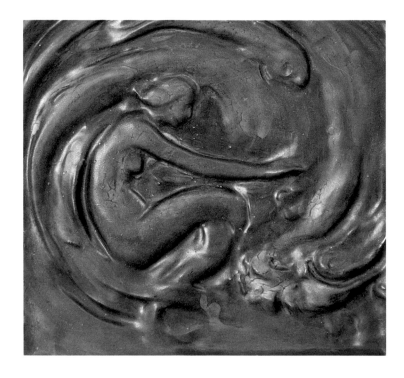

Upper left: FIREPLACE TILE, DINING ROOM
Lower left to right: STAINED GLASS, WEST DOOR;
DOOR DETAIL; COMMANDANT'S OFFICE

HALLWAY TO COMMANDANT'S OFFICE

THE WHITE PEACOCK

Next page: EASTERN MAPLE AND BEECH
BETWEEN LAWNS AND JAPANESE GARDEN

The Gardens

THE DUNSMUIR GARDENS WERE DESIGNED BY BRETT & HALL OF BOSTON AND BUILT
BETWEEN 1908 AND 1912 FOLLOWING THE CLASSIC PRINCIPLES OF THE EDWARDIAN
ENGLISH ESTATE, REGARDLESS OF COST OR NATURAL CONDITIONS. THE GARDENS HAVE
MATURED OVER THE PAST EIGHTY-FIVE YEARS WITH THE PATINA OF A LONG-PAST
ERA. GIANT COPPER BEECHES FLANK THE CASTLE ENTRANCE, AND THE NATIVE FOREST
HARKENS BACK TO A TIME BEFORE EUROPEANS SAILED TO THESE SHORES. THE
GARDENS HAVE REMAINED A LINK WITH THE PAST, A REMINDER OF AN ERA OF
GARDEN BOYS WASHING THE CLAY POTS AND HEAD GARDENERS PICKING GREENHOUSE
GRAPES AND ORCHIDS FOR THE TABLE.

Dave Rutherford
HEAD GARDENER, 1970-95

The Italian Garden

WISTERIA

LOGGIA IN AUTUMN

THE LOGGIA

WINTER

The Castle's gardens in winter offer an island of serenity and calm in the maelstrom of normal military and academic life swirling around them every day.

CAPT(N) A. T. (TONY) GOODE
COMMANDANT, 1984-87

DETAIL ON URN

STATUE REPRESENTING SPRING

SUMMER

AUTUMN

WINTER

The Japanese Garden

CHERRY BLOSSOMS

AZALEAS

SPRING RAIN

REFLECTIONS

RHODODENDRONS AND AZALEAS

PATH TO MIDDLE POND

STONE LANTERN AND AZALEAS

CAMELLIA PETALS

ORNAMENTAL HERON AND BRIDGE

STONE LANTERN

IRISES AND LAKE, SUMMER

PATH AROUND UPPER LAKE

BRIDGE TO ISLAND

JAPANESE MAPLE, AUTUMN

AUTUMN PATH

GINKGO LEAVES

JAPANESE MAPLE

THE BRIDGE IN WINTER

WINTER: SUN AND SNOW

The Forest

THE FOREST AT ROYAL ROADS IS PRECIOUS AND IRREPLACEABLE. THE FEELING OF IT IS
SOMETHING NEARLY IMPOSSIBLE TO PUT INTO WORDS. IT COMES FROM THE GREEN GLOW
EMANATING FROM BRACKEN FERN AND GIANT TREES, AND THE SWIFT SHADOW OF
THE OWL AS IT MELTS UPWARD INTO THE CANOPY. IT COMES FROM THE FUNGI OF THE
FOREST FLOOR IN FALL, FROM THE SEA OF SKUNK CABBAGES IN WET ALDER GROVES,
FROM THE WILDFLOWERS ON A WARM SPRING DAY. IT COMES FROM THE SOUND OF
COLWOOD CREEK AND THE MANY LITTLE SPRINGS, FROM COUNTLESS SONGBIRDS,
THE PILEATED WOODPECKER AND ANCIENT ECHOING CALL OF THE RAVEN.

Bev Hall
RESEARCH ASSISTANT, BIOLOGY 1982-95
PHOTOGRAPHER

MATURE CEDARS

FOREST CANOPY

UPPER SERPENTINE ROAD

FOREST TRAIL

AUTUMN

COLWOOD CREEK

A complete ecosystem, protected and tranquil: tall forests and beautiful gardens. We are so lucky to experience life in one of Canada's most prized estates. Let us hope that those who come after us will treat it with the care and dignity it deserves.

LT(N) CHRIS LYON
LECTURER IN MILITARY LEADERSHIP AND PSYCHOLOGY, 1992-95

COLWOOD CREEK, WINTER

SKUNK CABBAGES IN ALDER GROVE

BANANA SLUG AND MUSHROOM

FUNGUS IN AUTUMN

At times when the stresses of everyday living and working weighed heavily, a five-minute walk from the office placed us in the solitude of the forest, where the majesty of the evergreens and gentle sounds of birdsong and rushing water put our problems in perspective.

SHARON BELTON
ADMINISTRATIVE STAFF, 1984-95

Clockwise from upper left: TRILLIUM,
CAMAS, CALYPSO ORCHIDS
Previous page: EASTER LILIES

COAST BLACK TAIL DEER

My greatest moment was meeting and befriending Jasper, a beautiful white swan. It's amazing what you can learn from a bird.

20990 OFFICER CADET WENDY MORRISON
1993-95

MALLARDS

MALLARDS, ESQUIMALT LAGOON

GREAT BLUE HERON, ESQUIMALT LAGOON

Anyone who has served at Royal Roads cannot help but be touched by the majestic grandeur of its setting. This powerful image goes well beyond the surreal beauty of the grounds and is constantly manifested in the special bond and unique quality that link us all. Royal Roads' spirit will live on and continue to inspire generations of Canadians in the future.

COL CLAUDE NAUD
COMMANDANT, 1989-91

Chronology

COAST SALISH AND SONGHEES BANDS originally used the area around Esquimalt Lagoon, and part of the area was a burial ground. Archeological sites, most beside the lagoon, have been excavated and documented. Capt Cook and Capt Vancouver were in this vicinity in 1778 and 1794, but it was Sub-Lt Don Manuel Quimper who anchored in the roadstead in 1790, came ashore and claimed it for Carlos IV of Spain. (A roadstead is an area where ships can anchor safely near shore, though in less-sheltered conditions than within a harbour; "roads" is a short form, hence Royal Roads.) Several early settlers' enterprises were located on the property. A sawmill, tannery and shoe factory were established and fresh water from the springs was sold to the British Navy in nearby Esquimalt Harbour. The property was eventually bought by Roland Stuart, an Englishman who named the estate "Hatley Park."

1905   Fire destroys the original house on the grounds.

1907   James Dunsmuir, Vancouver Island coal industrialist and president of the E&N Railway, Premier of British Columbia (1900-02) and Lieutenant-Governor of the province (1906-09), acquires the first 600 acres of the property, and later adds other segments.

1908   The four-million-dollar house designed by Victoria architect Samuel Maclure is being built, and planning of the landscaping begins.

1910   Laura and James Dunsmuir move into Hatley Castle, still being completed.

1908-16   Rare and unusual trees, which are reaching maturity under heritage status in the 1990s, are imported and integrated into the landscape. A still-extant Black Hamburg grape vine, a slip taken from a 200-year-old vine at Hampton Court Palace, takes root in the Dunsmuir greenhouse, and what will become a venerable wisteria is planted in the gardens. Brett & Hall, a Boston firm, lays out the formal gardens. The Japanese Garden is designed by landscape architect Noda, from Japan.

1920   James Dunsmuir dies; his widow Laura continues living at the castle.

1940   The Government of the Dominion of Canada buys Hatley Park for $75,000, which is roughly the value of the fence surrounding the property. On December 13, HMCS *Royal Roads* is commissioned to train naval officers during World War II.

1941   Hatley Castle becomes a Naval Officer Training Establishment. Work begins to convert the dairy into an engineering school complete with lecture rooms, a draughting room and five fully equipped shops.

1942   On October 21, HMCS *Royal Roads* is "paid off" to make way for a new Royal Canadian Naval College. A two-year program is established to train naval officers. The Commandant's and Vice-Commandant's houses, plus a new cadet building – Grant Block – are completed. The stable is altered to provide eight classrooms and a gunnery school. A gymnasium, a boathouse and a wharf are under construction. The parade square is built on a levelled pasture between the Castle and Esquimalt Lagoon.

1947   The name of the college is changed from the Royal Canadian Naval College to the RCN-RCAF Joint Services College to reflect the combining of air force and navy training.

1948   The college is renamed Canadian Services College, Royal Roads, with army, navy and air force represented.

1954   Construction begins on Nixon Block (after Commander E.A.E. Nixon).

1955   The official opening of the Nixon Block is October 17.

1957   A swimming pool and squash courts are built.

1963   The first two pair of peacocks and peahens are presented by Mr. and Mrs. Fitzgerald of Penticton, and the resident flock begins its reign.

1968   The name of the college is officially changed from Canadian Services College, Royal Roads, to Royal Roads Military College (RRMC).

1973   The Minister of National Defence announces on July 13 that the college will expand to become a four-year institution.

1974   The award-winning Coronel Memorial Library is opened on November 1.

1975   The Royal Roads Military College Degree Act receives assent on June 26, allowing the college to grant degrees in its own name.

1976   The RRMC research launch *Tayut*, a 29-foot oceanographic instruction and research vessel, is delivered.

1977   The first graduation of a fourth-year class takes place in May.

1982   A new B.Sc. degree program in physics and computer science begins.

1984   Women begin training at the college as officer cadets. The Automatic Data Processing facility attached to Grant Block is completed in June.

1986   In May, the college is given the Freedom of the City of Victoria in recognition of its close association with the city over 46 years.

1987   The fine Edwardian estate is designated a federal heritage site. The first students are enrolled in postgraduate studies toward an M.Sc. in physical oceanography and acoustics. On May 10, the college is given the Freedom of the City of Colwood.

1990   Fiftieth Anniversary celebrations.

1991   The residential Millward wing of the Nixon Block is opened in May.

1994   The federal government announces on Tuesday, February 22 that Royal Roads Military College will close. By this time, degrees being granted include B.Sc. in physics, computer science, oceanography, earth observational science and applied military psychology, B.A. in military and strategic studies and in applied military psychology, and an M.Sc. in oceanography.

1995   On May 12-13, the final class graduates, and officer cadets receive their commissions.

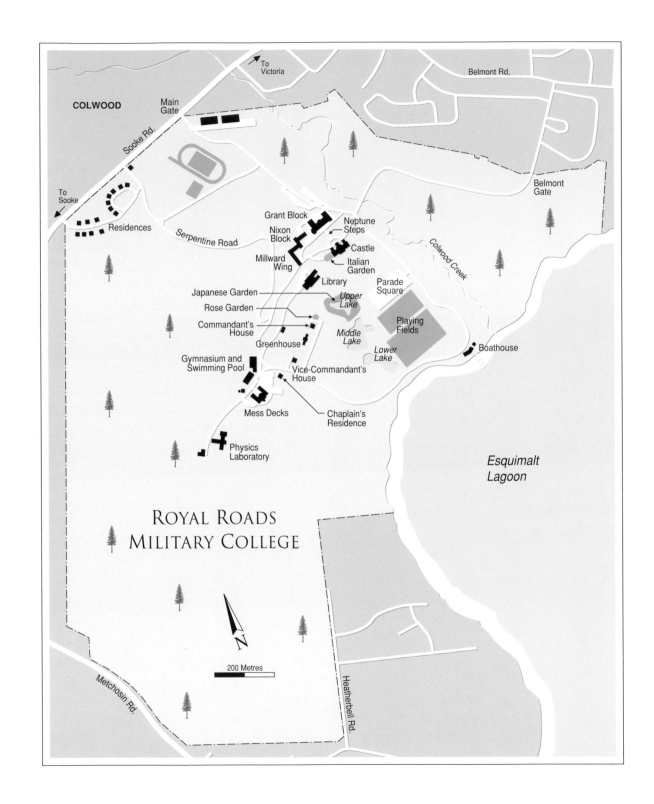

COLWOOD

To Victoria

Belmont Rd.

Main Gate

Sooke Rd.

Belmont Gate

To Sooke

Residences

Serpentine Road

Grant Block

Nixon Block

Millward Wing

Neptune Steps

Castle

Italian Garden

Colwood Creek

Library

Japanese Garden

Rose Garden

Commandant's House

Greenhouse

Upper Lake

Parade Square

Playing Fields

Middle Lake

Lower Lake

Boathouse

Gymnasium and Swimming Pool

Vice-Commandant's House

Mess Decks

Chaplain's Residence

Physics Laboratory

ROYAL ROADS
MILITARY COLLEGE

Esquimalt Lagoon

N

200 Metres

Metchosin Rd.

Heatherbell Rd.

Acknowledgements

GRATEFUL THANKS ARE EXTENDED to those within the Department of National Defence who over many years have kept Royal Roads in proud form. Owing to their careful stewardship, much of this Edwardian estate exists in virtually the same condition as when it was originally purchased from the Dunsmuir family in 1940.

We trust that the new provincial guardians in British Columbia will be just as fastidious in caring for this heritage property, a jewel facing pressures of change and urban growth.

We are also indebted to the following people for comments about their memories of Royal Roads, including some very appropriate quotations: BGen V. Michael Caines, LCol(Ret'd) George H. Herbert, BGen J. Harvey Roddick, Col K. Ross Betts, Col(Ret'd) George Logan, Capt (RCN)(Ret'd) R.C.K. (Bob) Peers, LCol(Ret'd) Dennis McCarthy, Col Claude Naud, Capt(N) A.J. (Tony) Goode, LCol(RCN)(Ret'd) Sid R. Wallace, LCol(Ret'd) James C. Parker, LCol Murray J. Haines, Maj(Ret'd) G.W. Stephen Brodsky, Maj Chris Hadfield, Lt(N) Chris Lyon, Dr. H. John Duffus, Dr. James A. Boutilier, Dr. G. Maurice Lancaster, Dr. Gerald A. Morgan, Dr. Dave W. Hone, Dr. Peter Smart, Dr. M.Ron Barr, Dr. W.T. (Bill) MacFarlane, Sharon Belton, Eileen Langstaff, Dave Rutherford, John Sheridan, Officer Cadets Mark Nasmith, Jason Toth, Andrew Chernysh, Danielle Rose, Barry Pitcher, Kael Rennie, Chris Scott, Wendy Morrison and Kathryn Hodgson. That more of the material they sent cannot be included verbatim is regrettable. Their encouragement has helped us enormously, and their quotes have been incorporated where possible.

The "Notes for Tour Guides" prepared by Claire Inkster and the anecdotal history written by Dr. Peter Dunnett, among other sources, have provided useful information about the history of the college.

Camilla Turner, our coordinating editor, deserves special praise and thanks for her reassuring guidance, cheerful countenance and incisive quill. She always seemed to have *le mot juste* when I was caught in a quagmire of cliché and hyperbole.

Tremendous moral support has been extended by the Registrar of RRMC, LCol(Ret'd) J.C. Parker and by the secretary-treasurer of the Vancouver Island branch of the Ex-Cadet Club, Ron Capern.

Some financial support has been provided by both the national and local bodies of the Ex-Cadet Club of Canada. Without their assistance, my bank manager might well have been hot on my case.

Finally, I would like to express my heartfelt gratitude to the Commandant of RRMC, Capt(N) Dave Bindernagel. Throughout this past year, which has been a most painful time in the College's history, he has been a source of strength and support for the civilian staff. Canada is fortunate to have leaders of his stature, and we are grateful for his assistance in doing everything he could to urge this book along.

M.G.R.
NATURAL LIGHT PRODUCTIONS

Photograph credits

MAURICE ROBINSON
Pages ii, viii, 2, 4, 8 (R), 9, 10 (L), 13, 15 (UR, LR), 16 (R), 17 (R), 18, 19, 20, 21, 22, 23, 26, 30, 33, 34, 35, 36 (LL), 39, 40, 41 (R), 42 (L), 43 (L), 44, 45, 46, 47 (UL, LR), 48, 49, 50 (UL, LL), 51, 52, 53, 55 (L), 60, 63 (R), 66 (L), 70 (R), 71 (R), 76 (R), 79, 81, 84, 86 (L), 87 (L), 90, 91, 93 (UR), 94, 95 (R), 97, 104

BEVERLEY HALL
Pages vi, 3, 6, 7, 8 (L), 10 (R), 12, 14 (L), 15 (L), 16 (L), 17 (L), 24 (R), 25, 27, 28, 29, 31, 32, 37, 38, 41 (L), 42 (R), 43 (LR), 47 (UR,LL), 55 (UR, LR), 56, 57, 58, 59, 61, 64, 65, 67, 68, 69, 70 (L), 71 (L), 73, 75, 77, 78, 80, 82, 83, 85, 86 (R), 87 (R), 88, 89, 92, 93 (UL, LR), 95 (L), 96, 98, 99

PAUL PRICE
Pages 11, 14 (R), 36 (UL, R), 43 (UR), 50 (LM, LR), 54, 62, 63 (L), 66 (R), 72, 74, 76 (L)

DARREN OXNER (COLLEGE PHOTOGRAPHER)
Pages 5, 24 (L)

Key: **R** (RIGHT); **L** (LEFT); **UR** (UPPER RIGHT); **LR** (LOWER RIGHT); **UL** (UPPER LEFT); **LL** (LOWER LEFT); **LM** (LOWER MIDDLE)